RE ◀◀
DEFINED

A 21 DAY REFLECTIVE JOURNEY TO
REFRAMING THE WAY YOU THINK ABOUT
EVERYDAY LIFE DECISIONS

Dr. LaQuenta Long

REDEFINED

Copyright © 2022 Dr. LaQuenta Long

The content of this book is for informational purposes only and is not intended to diagnose, treat, cure, or prevent any condition or disease. You understand that this book is not intended as a substitute for consultation with a licensed practitioner. Please consult with your own physician or healthcare specialist regarding the suggestions and recommendations made in this book. The use of this book implies your acceptance of this disclaimer.

All rights reserved. No part of this publication may be reproduced, stored in a retrieval system, stored in a database and / or published in any form or by any means, electronic, mechanical, photocopying, recording or otherwise, without the prior written permission of the author. Please do not participate in or encourage piracy of copyrighted materials in violation of the author's rights. Purchase only authorized editions.

Table of Contents

Introduction   5

Redefined: A 21 Day Reflective Journey to Reframing the Way You Think About Everyday Life Decisions 7

1	Layers	8
2	Shift Your Focus	12
3	Sometimes Your New Beginning Doesn't Start at the Beginning: At Least Not the Beginning You Are Thinking	16
4	Dealing with Distractions	20
5	You Can't Run Someone Else's Race	23
6	What does it take to make a change?	26
7	Dream Big! What Does It Mean to You?	29
8	Who Are You Trying to Get to Understand You?	32
9	Success Is an Inner Process	35
10	Are You Willing to Do the Work?	38

11	Embracing the Lonely Seasons	41
12	Facing Yourself	45
13	Achieving Your Maximum, Not Your Minimum	48
14	Yes to Your Potential	52
15	What Are You Waiting For?	55
16	Avoidance Doesn't Produce Change	58
17	Sacrificing the Present for the Future	61
18	Guarding Your Vision	64
19	Respecting the Process	68
20	Addressing Vulnerability	72
21	What Does It Mean to Be More Intentional?	76
Journaling		**80**

INTRODUCTION

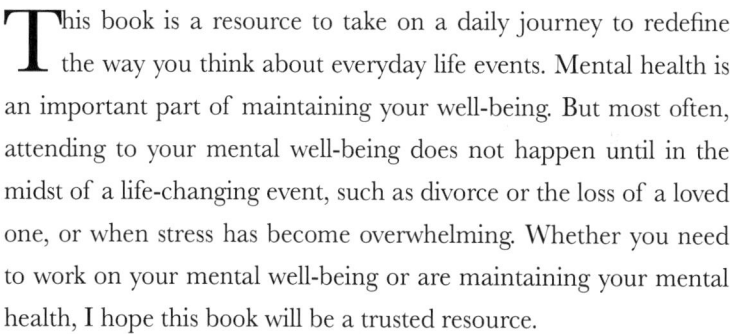

This book is a resource to take on a daily journey to redefine the way you think about everyday life events. Mental health is an important part of maintaining your well-being. But most often, attending to your mental well-being does not happen until in the midst of a life-changing event, such as divorce or the loss of a loved one, or when stress has become overwhelming. Whether you need to work on your mental well-being or are maintaining your mental health, I hope this book will be a trusted resource.

The goal of the next 21 days is to get you in the practice of being reflective on the way you think about certain things in your life. To challenge you to identify problem-solving approaches that address the problem at hand and not be overwhelmed by the task of addressing it. To consider the relationships in your life and better ways of taking care of them.

There are 21 readings to support a 30-day cycle of reflecting on how you are making the changes outlined. It is helpful if the things that resonate with you that need to be changed have some space for accountability. The tasks here are awareness and action. Once you have read through all the devotions, go back through and revisit how you are implementing the changes you are looking to make.

I encourage you to use this book in one of two ways. First, you might commit to reading one a day, reviewing the tips at the end of the reading, and taking a reflective journey of your mindset around the subject for that day. Each day finding clarity, accountability, and a refresher of how you think about things. Moving through each day a little closer to being more intentional in the ways you think and manage the day-to-day things.

The second way you may use this book is to take a reading at a time and work on mastering how you use the tips in your everyday life. Some things may require you to ponder on them a little longer. You may work to master the changes you decide to make in the topic discussed.

The aim of this book is to slow down long enough to consider your mindset, taking time to consider how you are doing and thinking about something and how you want to continue doing it. Mental health is an important part of your overall well-being. Incorporating simple ways to be accountable to taking care of it can have a lasting impact on how you cope.

Redefined: A 21 Day Reflective Journey to Reframing the Way You Think About Everyday Life Decisions

1
Layers

I want to ask you a question today about self-worth. What layers have you clothed yourself with to hide how you truly feel about yourself? Self-worth is how you define your value. Now, some of you might already wear "garments" that match your self-worth, but I find most often this is not the case, even for the most successful of people. Here is something I would encourage you to consider: Do the garments you are wearing demonstrate self-worth, or are the garments in place to take care of who you are?

Real-talk moment: Clothing should take care of you, not define you.

Let's go a little further with this thought.

You might put on undergarments to portray feelings of security and support. Next, you put on a shirt to reflect your personality and style. Pants to demonstrate poise and how you carry yourself into a room. Maybe you add a jacket to demonstrate power and control over your circumstances. You select a pair of shoes to indicate the arena of life you play in. All the while, underneath, you can hide who you truly are because the garments are there to speak for you. And nobody needs to know what you feel inside.

But here is the naked truth. No matter the garments you put on, if you don't value yourself, the garments become heavy. Your gait shifts.

How about we switch gears and talk about the garments you wear when you know your self-worth. You select garments that take care of who you are. Your undergarments are not just for security and support but for comfort and flexibility for what the day has in store. You choose a shirt reflective of what you plan to do for the day, whether business, leisure, or play. You slip on pants that are protective of the elements the day may produce. A jacket is only worn when the occasion supports its use. The way you dress says, "I planned for the day." Choices are selected to ensure endurance for the task at hand. Notice the shift in what you decide to layer yourself in. The focus is not on what others see but on what you plan to do for the day.

Let's put this example to the side for a moment and just talk about self-worth. Self-worth is your value, and no one else but you determines it. Once you have decided the definition of who you are, the script of how you live it out can be written.

I want you to take this reflective journey with me. Try the steps below. Take an intentional step toward the person and the life you seek to live.

Steps:

1. Write out the defining points of value for who you are. This is not a statement of what you have accomplished; it's about the person you want to be. It is about the kind of person you represent amid anything life has in store. For example,

"I am determined, driven, and dependable. I am supposed to have good in my life." "I am loving and kind. I represent this in everything I am connected to." "I am chilled and laid back. I am about living life." "I am about keeping peace in the things I do. I encourage detailed statements." You are more than one thing; you are a summary of traits. For now, just focus on a couple and then later choose a couple more to expand your definition.

2. Write how you would like this to show up in the life you live. In work, home, leisure. How would others know this about you? This would be represented by actions and not words. How you carry yourself. What you choose to do in a day. How you tend to the things of the day.

3. Last, write about the things you would have to layer yourself with to take care of who you are. Would you have to learn new skills to increase security and support, to feel more comfortable and flexible with who you are? What activities can you connect to that reflect your self-worth? Understand that the layers are not meant to cover up your worth but to take care of it.

Self-worth is yours to define.

2
Shift Your Focus

Do you ever find yourself thinking about why something has happened? Or beating yourself up over what you should have done? Or maybe you look at yourself and wish you could be different somehow. There are countless ways this way of thinking may show up in your life. Thoughts that occur minute by minute, hour by hour, day by day. Many times, you find yourself stuck in this pattern of thought, and you decide this is just what it is. Hopelessness or discouragement can set in as you consider how to live with your thoughts. Now, I am not looking to have you in a place of despair but a place of honesty. A place of awareness that you are not alone in. I have often told my clients that I tend to go to the worst-case scenario first. It is something that started when I was young. The "why" of this pattern is not the part we focus on because sometimes, knowing the "why" is not the creator of change. Today, I am going to encourage you on what to do when it happens. Because no matter where you are in your healing journey from the why, addressing what is happening in the here and now changes the course you are on at this moment.

So, what do you do when your thoughts don't reflect where you want to be, what you think, or how you want to feel? Simply put—it is in shifting your focus. The method in and of itself is simple. The idea is to change the thought you are focusing on. In a healthy state of thinking, we can do this, no problem. We could look up at the sky and see that it is blue. Someone could ask what else you see, and you would say clouds or a plane flying or look around and see trees and houses. You could shift your focus from the blue sky you first focused on and see that there is so much more than just that one thing.

The challenge in this simple method comes from how long you stare at one thing. Have you ever looked into something bright, even for just a moment? Your vision can be blurred and disoriented, even if you have stopped looking at it. Now just imagine that you prolonged the look into that bright light for more than seconds. The length of time for your sight to recover is prolonged. You would be able to recognize shapes and outlines of things, but it is not until you close your eyes for a moment to reset and rest that your eyes begin to recover. You're no longer straining them in efforts to gain sight. After time passes, you can open them, and you begin to find yourself looking around and seeing things. You're able to see more clearly.

Here is what I want you to take away from this. Shifting your focus is not always just about changing what you are looking at. Sometimes it requires you to close your eyes and take a moment of rest from the strain to see things clearly.

Tips:

1. Closing your eyes. This represents a couple of things. One, it's a place of rest. A place where you give yourself a timeout from working so hard to change. It's not that you have stopped working on the change, but you are giving

yourself the energy needed to make the change. Two, it represents closing down from seeing all the options around you. Sometimes too many options can be overwhelming and just as discouraging as having no options.

2. Opening your eyes. Understand that after you rest and reset your eyes, it is important to take in the things you now see differently once you open your eyes. Take note of the things you missed before. Because in doing so, it will be easier for you to consider their existence if you ever find yourself focusing on the wrong things in the future.

3

Sometimes Your New Beginning Doesn't Start at the Beginning: At Least Not the Beginning You Are Thinking

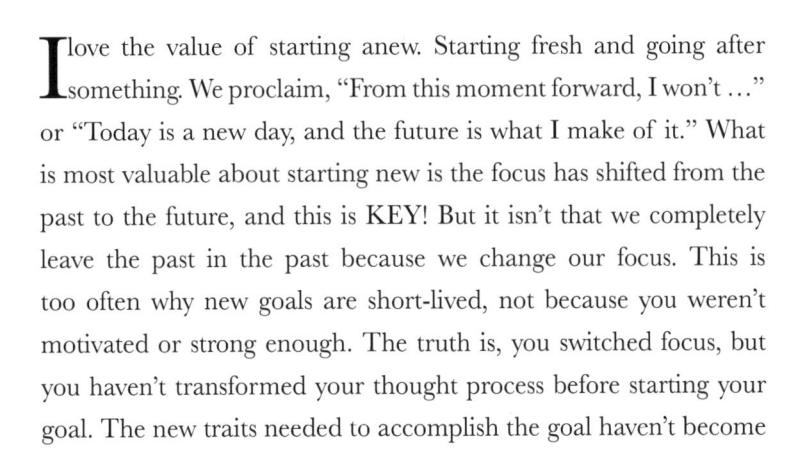

I love the value of starting anew. Starting fresh and going after something. We proclaim, "From this moment forward, I won't …" or "Today is a new day, and the future is what I make of it." What is most valuable about starting new is the focus has shifted from the past to the future, and this is KEY! But it isn't that we completely leave the past in the past because we change our focus. This is too often why new goals are short-lived, not because you weren't motivated or strong enough. The truth is, you switched focus, but you haven't transformed your thought process before starting your goal. The new traits needed to accomplish the goal haven't become part of your default system yet.

So, if your new beginning doesn't start at the beginning, you might wonder, where does it start?

It starts with addressing what tripped you up in the past and what worked for you. Call it your prerequisite for change. It's that bit of knowledge and training you need just before getting started.

When you start a new job. It's understood, for the most part, you were hired because you were qualified for the position. However, new companies don't usually start someone before sending them through orientation. A new hire usually goes through orientation, training, and a period where they may work alongside someone until they can confidently do most of the work on their own. It is understood that being qualified doesn't mean you automatically know how to navigate the new workplace. You may have to change the way you do things to fit your new workplace, or you may have to fine-tune old ways of doing things. Are you getting the picture?

You are qualified and ready for the new place you desire to go. But all you are familiar with is the old habits, the old situations, the old way of doing things. Your response and style need to be trained for where you plant yourself next and the new way of doing things. So here are a couple of things I want you to consider:

1. Consider what was working before. Make a list, reflect on why these things worked, and then be patient with the process of acclimating to the new ways in which you will use them. If it is your personality or energy that you bring to something, give space for others to get to know you and give yourself time to learn who they are. Don't abandon what was working before; just understand new ways in which you can use those tools.

2. Realize what wasn't working. This doesn't always involve letting go completely but understanding why it wasn't working. It might fit in with your new goals, with only minor adjustments needed. But if you find that it is not working in your new space, then it is time to let it go and try something new.
3. Take time to learn. New places will always provide an opportunity for growth. Don't shy away from it. You are capable, but it takes some time. Remember the value of why you are on your new course to this new place and that anything you are learning with practice and persistence will one day not be so hard to do. But you have to be willing to do the work and stay the course.

Your new beginning is worth taking the time to be ready for.

4

Dealing with Distractions

I think the topic of distraction is very relatable. Distractions are constant and ever-present, but we must deal with them to truly accomplish anything. I have rules of thumb I will share with you that have aided me in accomplishing most things in my life.

First, you must know what distracts you and what areas of your life these things show up in. Distractions can be for a season, or they can be constant. A seasonal one might be the desire to have a spouse or children. You might find yourself at work thinking about this. You might be in conversation with a friend, and your mind wanders to this. A constant distraction might be something like having the thought "I am not good enough," so you are constantly trying to find ways to become good enough. Whatever the distraction is, you must identify it as such so you can address it.

Second, understand whether the distraction has a place in your life. The distraction I commonly have is my creative side. I will come up with an idea in the midst of working on something else. And I will want to detour to that idea. While the idea might be good and relevant, at that moment, it's a distraction. This isn't something I need to completely cut out, but it is something I have to address to complete anything. Feelings of not being enough can be a distraction, but they also might be something to learn from. Distractions you might need to cut out are things that are not relevant in this season of your life. While there may be value in having children if you are in the midst of transitions, such as a new career or school, it might be a distraction that you have to set aside to accomplish what you are presently working on. The point is we can often justify distractions at the moment, but we have to learn to manage them. The more you understand what they are and how they show up, the better you will become in getting back on track.

Tips

1. Know what distracts you. Take at least a week to write down the things that take you off track. Note the types of things you were doing when you got distracted.

2. Identify whether the distraction has a place in your life presently. If it does, figure out how and where it more appropriately should show up to not be a distraction. Once you do this, you can give yourself permission to take care of it later because you have created a space for it to show up productively.

3. If the distraction you identify doesn't have a place right now, determine whether there is a future place for it or whether you need to dismiss the distraction entirely.

5

You Can't Run Someone Else's Race

You can't run someone else's race. This powerful truth is not a new thought but one you may not always feel accountable for. Countless times, I have heard people say to me, "But I am not you!" I have heard it said to me, and I have thought it about others. But here is the thing: I am not supposed to be anyone else but me. And you are not supposed to be anyone else but you. So why do we get trapped in the cycles of comparing? One thought I will talk about here has to do with what the other person has been or is currently achieving or at least what you *perceive* they are achieving. Now don't get me wrong; other things also influence the comparison game. But for the purpose of this conversation, we will center on this one piece of the puzzle.

When you focus on what someone has achieved or is presently doing, you lose sight of the journey that got them there. The comparison is in where you are in this moment and not the distance to where they are now. It may seem as though that person magically appeared in their present situation, which makes your statement of "not being them" feel a lot more valid. When I say you can't run someone else's race, it is with the understanding that the race itself is the important part. And it is filled with everything that makes the results that much better. When you look to run someone else's race, you frustrate the process of becoming the better version of yourself. The skills you need to handle the results are underdeveloped, and the results don't always align with where you should be.

I want to offer you a different perspective.

1. Take time to understand the significance of what you see them doing or having that you value. Sometimes it is not the actual thing that matters the most; it is what you believe is happening as a result of it. For example, friends who are in a healthy marriage; the value might be in not having to be alone or feeling like you are someone a person could love or any other number of things. Taking the time to recognize it helps you see what you really need to focus on and strive for.

2. Consider what it took for that person to achieve results. Whether you believe it or not, it took effort for that person to be where they are, and it takes effort to maintain it. Doing this helps normalize the idea that if you are willing to commit to the journey, it is possible to achieve the same results.

3. Consider what it takes for you personally to get from where you are in this moment to the results you desire. Sometimes the path will be shorter, and sometimes it will be longer. The value is your growth in the process. The value is in your self-awareness along the way, which will make your success even sweeter.

6
WHAT DOES IT TAKE TO MAKE A CHANGE?

Most of us recognize when something in our life needs to change. Something tells us that we can't stay where we are. But change comes with many unknowns, and sometimes there are many questions about how to change. This can stop, delay, or derail us from the path that leads to change. Being caught up in our feelings can keep us from making the necessary changes in our lives.

So what does it take to change? Focus on the WHY! Your WHY helps you focus on the benefits of change. It's the fuel that motivates you to make the change. More than likely, you are already taking steps toward change. Now it's time to finish what you started. It's time to make it happen.

Tips

1. Take some time to visualize what benefits can come from change. Visualize what change will mean for you, your

family, and those close to you. Think about how you will learn and grow as a result of the change. Take note of these things. These form your WHY.

2. Consider the resources you already possess to make this change. This list may include characteristics, traits, skills, people, and more. Once you clearly understand the resources you already have, then you will discover where the gaps lie and how to fill them in.

3. Identify what you need for accountability. Anything you do that requires you to stretch or step into the unfamiliar requires some level of accountability, no matter how strong and determined you are. Accountability can be a resource. Someone or something that keeps you moving forward reminds you of your why and encourages you in moments of fatigue. So make sure there is accountability in place.

Dream Big! What Does It Mean to You?

Whether we realize it or not, "dreaming big" is a vague concept to consider. It can mean different things depending on who you are. What does it mean to you to "dream big"? Is it just a simple concept that I am overthinking? I want you to keep reading and allow me to share what I mean.

For some, to "dream big" means to overcome. "I have to overcome all the things I've been through." "I have to overcome the past, my failures, the things people have said about me, the things I have said about myself!" In this instance, to "dream big" is not about the dream. It is about dismantling everything you know to be true and seeing something different.

For someone else, "dreaming big" means access. "I have to find the things I need to achieve." Is your dream beyond your current resources?

Maybe the "dream" is drowning in comparisons. "Can I do it better than others?" Once again, it's not the dream that matters. It's how well you match up to someone else's capabilities. To "dream big" results in constant disappointment because you're never good enough.

Get what I mean now? That dreaming big could mean different things? It may not even be about the dream at all, but about what you have to move through to dream big. Dreaming big is met with roadblocks. And those roadblocks are personal to you.

The more you know about what holds you up from dreaming big, the more you can address it and free yourself to go after the Big Dreams.

Tips.

1. Take note. Take note of things you think about when it comes to your next-level aspirations. Stepping out of your comfort zone, what are you saying to yourself? What are the responses of others around you? These are things that are holding you back and must be addressed if you want to dream big easily.

2. Create safeguards. Dreaming big is easy, but there are things in your life that seek to rob you of that dream. The thieves come in many shapes and forms. Identify things that help safeguard your dream.

3. Give grace. This is for you in the process. As you work toward dreaming big, working through steps one and two, it will get easier. But it's not a perfect process. Giving yourself grace helps you to respect the process.

8
WHO ARE YOU TRYING TO GET TO UNDERSTAND YOU?

There is an overwhelming desire for others to understand who you are, why you operate the way you do, and what influences you to make the choices you make. A lot of time and energy is given to making people understand you. Don't get me wrong; there is a time and place for that. But the reality is it doesn't require as much time as you give it. And certain people don't have to understand you!

Let's look at why someone should understand the "behind the scenes" of how you think, feel, operate in life. You may want someone to understand you because they are influenced by how you do things. You may want someone to understand you because you will work with them on a task for an extended period. But outside these two considerations, there is unlikely to be a need for someone else to understand who you are and why you do what you do.

So why would you push for understanding from irrelevant people? I am going to share something, but I want you to slow down long enough to consider what I say. I want you to take time to remove yourself from defense and be reflective. Ok, here it goes. The work you put into getting others to understand you has more to do with your own insecurity than the need for them to understand.

Insecurity is when you waver in your decisions. Insecurity shows up when you try new things. Insecurity is when you tried before and failed. Insecurity is when you desire someone else to affirm what you are thinking or feeling. When you find yourself in those insecurities, you over-explain. You look for approval. You change your mind frequently.

Truth be told, the person whom you need to understand you is YOU. You are the key person. You are the primary person. When you are secure in YOU from one moment to the next, you can better filter out the people you need to understand you. So, if you find yourself looking for someone else to understand you, take time to search out possible insecurities so you can strengthen your confidence in this area.

Tips

1. Insecurities are not always bad. Insecurities occur for all kinds of reasons. Recognizing them gives you a place to grow and self-correct the things that need to change. Embrace insecurities—they are a part of the journey. Then put in the work to correct them.

2. Don't try to address everything you notice at once. Grow and change one thing. This will create a ripple effect. Find the thing that is slowing you down the most, that affects you emotionally, the thing that you give way too much time thinking about and keeps you from doing other things. Then, step by step, do the work to change.

9

Success Is an Inner Process

I was listening to a motivational video, and one of the speakers defined success as an inner process. This resonated with me. "Success is an inner process." So I did a Google search for the definition of success to see how it is technically defined. And the first thing that popped up said success is "the accomplishment of aim or purpose." With these two things in mind, I want to share something that will hopefully have you thinking about success differently.

If success is an inner process, and you are successful when you accomplish the thing you aim for, then success can be achieved every time you go after something because the achievement has to do with YOU, not with what you actually achieve. We often associate success with a feeling. We want to feel successful. Success is not on the spectrum of feelings you can have. It is an experience. It is an experience that you have within yourself. It is hard to have this experience when you set your aim on something you have limited control over.

Here is a truthful moment. When you don't think you can achieve success, you are less likely to strive for it. We all want to experience success, but being successful doesn't have to mean "being the best." "Being the best" is fleeting, especially when you are always the best and never challenged.

The experience of success is best felt when you know what you have accomplished is something that you strived for. Success is found in the effort you give to be your best. And when you consider what it took to create your best, it comes from an internal place.

I encourage you to switch your focus to internal successes. Success should be an ongoing experience, not a brief, fleeting moment.

Tips

1. Figure out a goal you are working toward, a project you have coming up, a trait you are trying to improve upon. Once you have that one thing in mind, think about the characteristics, skills, and effort it will take to make it happen. List these things and identify where you are at presently. Once you have identified these things, they become your true measure of success. (As you work to achieve your best in these, they will influence the accomplishment of your goal. The difference is that your experience of success is not limited by achieving the goal.)

10

ARE YOU WILLING TO DO THE WORK?

Are you willing to do the work? This is an "Ouch" kind of question. When it is something that has value or significance, your default answer wants to be yes. But what happens when the answer is truly no? It will show up in your effort, motivation, and quality. There is a difference between willingness and ability.

Ability reflects your capabilities to do something. It can be that you have the time, the skills, and the knowledge to accomplish a task. If you have the ability, sometimes it is difficult to see yourself saying no.

Willingness, on the other hand, may have nothing to do with ability. Willingness reflects your desire, your drive, your motivation. It is the openness to stretch yourself beyond your limitations. Willingness is not about skills; it's about heart.

Asking and answering this question doesn't have to come from a place of judgment. Instead, let it be from one of accountability. Let it be reflective. At the end of the day, you may still end up doing the work, but there is a truthfulness you can have reflecting on why your effort may not always be the same in all of your endeavors. Your communication around how much time you put in something can come from an honest place versus a defensive one. Understanding the importance of willingness can explain why you say no when it seems like everything else supports you saying yes.

Are you willing to do the work? This can be an empowering question you can use to check your heart for the work at hand instead of relying only on your abilities.

Tips

1. Measure the task at hand beyond what it will take in tangible ways (time, skill, resources) to complete it. Look at how it would feel to participate in it and the results that come out of it. Look for impact in your overall purpose. How would you feel sacrificing other things of value to complete this task?

2. Try to understand if the work will require you to be engaged for a long- or short-term basis. Your heart and abilities might easily sync to accomplish a short-term commitment. That may not be so when it comes to long-term commitments. Never underestimate what it means to be willing, especially when we commit to being in a workspace for a long time.

11

Embracing the Lonely Seasons

Some individuals like to keep their social circle small and simple. Others keep their social circles big and wide. No matter which way you are designed, sometimes the circle includes only one person, YOU. The adjustment to being ONE can be uncomfortable. It may cause you to question WHY you are alone. But a season of ONE can have significance to a season of change.

Let's talk about some of the valuable things that can happen during seasons in which you feel lonely. The seasons where access to your circle of friends, circle of supporters, circle of family, whatever that circle is, is limited.

Seasons where this happens can often represent a change you are going through, where you are professionally (such as a change in companies, change in position, change in the industry). With this kind of change, you are not only getting used to the newness of the job but also the newness of your coworkers. Or maybe work responsibilities limit your ability to participate in social events like you used to.

Some seasons have to do with personal life changes, such as getting married, having kids, or the loss of a loved one. This kind of season has you shifting your focus to learn the ropes of new responsibilities along with the old. Sometimes, these new changes no longer match the social scene you used to be a part of.

Other seasons of loneliness can be brought about because of changes you are making within yourself, such as personal healing, understanding your past, or a personal desire for change. In a season like this, there are things you learn that you may not be able to discuss with your social circle. You need time with yourself more than you need time with others.

Whichever route leads you to a season of loneliness, it does not have to turn into a negative situation. It is just different. It does not have to be forever; it is just a season.

I encourage embracing a season of loneliness. I have been described as a social butterfly, and I have had my share of lonely seasons. I personally don't love seasons where I don't have access to my circle, but I have learned to value what can be done in them. So the tips I will share are meant to help you utilize these seasons effectively. They are not about diminishing the value of your social circle.

Tips

1. Identify what you could be doing to better yourself and your circumstances while your social circle is small. Often, these events require adjustments, but they are worth the energy it takes to make the adjustment.

2. Become comfortable with the notion that sometimes your circle experiences life changes. If you are newly married, sometimes you can't do the things your single friends can keep doing. If you have taken on administrative roles in your company, you may have to change your relationship with co-workers. This doesn't mean your social circles are less important; it just means that your role within them may have to be adjusted.
3. Remember that seasons of loneliness are an experience. They are primarily defined by your interpretation of them. Writers may isolate themselves to write. College students will isolate themselves to focus on their studies. New moms focus on their newborns. It's OK to shift your focus; the importance is in understanding why it is happening and how to convey the changes to your social circles.

12
Facing Yourself

Sometimes, the person you see in the mirror does not reflect who you really are. To face yourself, you have to change the way you see yourself. Too often, we rely heavily on our outward image. "If I dress better, I will see myself as successful, and so will others." "If I get this job, then I will have significance." "Once I get married, I won't see myself as unattractive or undesirable."

I remember one year I commented to myself that people came to see me as a therapist not because of how I dressed but because of what was in my mind and how it helped them. At that moment, I spent less time on my image; my focus was no longer fragmented. I became more relaxed, and the depth of my appointments improved. What I did at that moment empowered the version of myself that mattered most. I could focus on the parts that helped me thrive professionally. It became outwardly apparent that I had changed. That doesn't mean I all-of-a-sudden stopped thinking about how I dressed. I still placed value in looking professional. But I no longer assigned value to myself professionally based on my dress.

Facing yourself is all about shifting focus from what you see outwardly. It's about not being overly concerned with what others think. It is about working on what you think about yourself—how to strengthen the mental image you have of yourself. It is in defining yourself with the characteristics, traits, and styles that shape the outward image.

Tips

1. Instead of looking into a physical mirror, I want you to close your eyes and describe what you see. I want you to describe not just physical attributes but go deeper. Describe the traits you possess—what you think people see when they see you. It's about facing your insecurities and acknowledging areas where you are successful. Once you have done this, determine what you want to maintain, what you want to transform, and what you want to let go of.

2. If it is challenging for you to identify both the good and bad traits, take some time to describe the "future you." The person you want to be. Once you have this image, daily close your eyes and repeat this new list of descriptors to yourself. And then commit to yourself one thing you will work toward that day to improve.

Working on yourself is an ongoing process. And sometimes, it takes a while to own a part of yourself that seems disconnected. But each day you work on it, you close the gap.

13

Achieving Your Maximum, Not Your Minimum

When you consider what to go after in life, do you consider the bare minimum, or do you consider all that is possible? Would you tell the child version of yourself only to strive for "just enough," or would you encourage them to go after their heart's desire? Truth be told, even with me asking you in this manner, there may be some hesitation in answering that you would go after the maximum.

Why is it that just enough seems to be where you land? Why is it that "comfortable" becomes sufficient? Why is going after the ideal dream so far-fetched?

Let's talk about truths for a minute.

Sometimes the dream is not one you've designed for yourself, and some dreams do not create passion inside you. Instead of adding value to your life, the dream is more about status. While status dreams are not bad, they just don't always match what it means to live your maximum life. If you find yourself in this situation, you do not have to stay there.

Maximum living has to do with a combination of everything that represents your life being well-lived. Maximum living means that several areas in your life come together to produce the best possible life for you.

Think about your favorite song.

It is a mix of great lyrics, great melody, a great beat, and vocal tones that go high and low. Without one of these components, the song is not the same. Your maximum living involves how you live your home life, professional life, and personal life. It is becoming the best version of you in ALL aspects.

I encourage you to look at the different areas of your life and determine whether you have settled because it is familiar. Or is it truly representative of how you want to live? If it is a relationship, are you guys just going through the motions, or is it time to go on more dates, heal the broken parts, or try something new together? If it is your professional life, are you just showing up without wanting to be there? Maybe it's not going after a new job position. Sometimes it's a matter of bringing the passion back to what you are already doing. Or maybe it is inspiring and teaching others about what you do or being a better co-worker. Whatever steps you need to take, the point is to stretch yourself to live your best life.

Tips

1. Be reflective. Living your maximum life is not always about going after something different than what you have.

Sometimes it is about getting better at it. Often when someone is asked about goals, the focus shifts to school or work goals. Your life represents so much more than what you do in these areas. So, in your reflection, think about whether more quality time with family is relevant; think about self-care and self-interest; think about job performance; think about learning new things. And when you find there is something more you can do, start working toward making improvements.

2. Recognize some changes are a marathon, not a sprint. Some changes are made quickly, such as going out on dates with your spouse. Or taking time to read a book. Or showing up at work and being more involved. Other changes take more time. Like when you need to heal broken parts of a relationship. When you need to learn to look at yourself differently, or when you start something new. Determining the speed at which you change is just as important as knowing what you need to change; it influences your performance. Change can be hard; don't be afraid to ask for help.

14
Yes to Your Potential

Saying yes to your potential is about showing up each day and giving it your ALL; it's seeing that you have potential in the first place and knowing there is always more you can achieve. Saying yes to your potential is not being so complacent in the good that you miss out on the great.

To say yes to your potential, you also must dispel the lies and distractions you tell yourself and the ones that others tell you. Some say you should settle for "good enough" because most would love to have what you have. They tell you to not think too highly of yourself and to change who you are. These are distractions and noise that keep you bound to what IS instead of pursuing what could BE.

Saying yes to your potential is a significant part of living. It's the part that promotes growth. Growth in you personally, growth in your family, growth professionally. When you say yes, it requires you to learn new things, build up strength and endurance, and be accountable. But you can do it with the right resources.

Tips

1. Ask yourself if there is an area of your life that you are expanding beyond what is comfortable and familiar. It is not just about the big things; it's about the little things as well. It could be reading a book or going to a seminar and learning something new. It could be a new health goal to eat better. Or it could be the job promotion. The idea is not to be complacent.

2. Understand the difference between being appreciative of what you have and the desire for more. Going after your potential is not about minimizing all that you already have. It is about knowing there is always more available. Write out every thought you associate with going after your potential. Label whether it promotes you to move forward or stay put. If it is something you don't like, seek to understand why you think this way and then replace it with a new thought.

15
What Are You Waiting For?

Sometimes, the "waiting game" can get in the way of your accomplishments. The idea that you need to wait for certain things to happen before you can accomplish your goals or that everything has to be in place before you can go after your dreams can hold you back.

Here is the truth. It is rare if ever that life presents the perfect circumstances.

The value is in making the decision and then navigating things that are presently happening, preparing for potential problems, and adjusting for the unexpected.

Waiting to get started puts unnecessary delays in the time it takes to achieve. Delays will occur. I want to challenge you to analyze the reasons why you are waiting. Will waiting support your goal? Or are you holding back because of uncertainty?

Waiting as a resource means you are actually doing something in this period. You are saving money; you are learning or improving on a skill; you are networking. In this situation, waiting is part of the process. However, if you're waiting because of uncertainty, time can be spent worrying about "what if," wavering on whether it is right or not, or listening to others' opinions. This type of waiting keeps you questioning versus addressing the issues to move you forward.

I encourage you to ask yourself: "What am I waiting for"? If you realize that your waiting is delaying action, it's time to switch gears. Time to decide and start moving forward.

Tips

1. What is influencing your waiting period the most? Unpack all the things you are considering. Address their validity. If they are valid concerns, then you need to consider changing directions or try and figure out ways to address them. Once you start addressing them, you are no longer in a waiting period. You are taking steps to make things happen.

2. Determine if you need to implement deadlines. Sometimes you can fool yourself into thinking you are actively working on something when you are really just delaying the next step. If you are not actively working, you are waiting. Sometimes you will need accountability.

16

Avoidance Doesn't Produce Change

Have you ever experienced poor customer service and thought to yourself, "I'm NEVER coming back here"? Or maybe you had difficulty learning or completing a task, so you decide it is not for you. You may be experiencing "avoidance."

Avoidance can bring a temporary resolution to a circumstance, but it does not produce change. The reality is whatever you are avoiding is still there. What you are avoiding may show up in other situations, and instead of feeling insecure in one area, these feelings might show up in other areas. It could also be your perception of a situation. You leave one job because you couldn't trust the people you were working with only to find yourself feeling the same way about your new co-workers.

True change comes when you deal with the situation or person at hand. Sometimes you can do this by simply having a conversation, or maybe change involves taking time to learn new strategies. But most often, the work is internal. Having to address the emotion or thought that lingers from past experiences.

Do not underestimate the work this involves. The benefits far outweigh the energy you will expend as you make changes.

When you avoid things, you place limitations on your life. By addressing things and not avoiding them, you start to give yourself new hope and new opportunities.

Tips

1. Identify an area of avoidance. Understand what is connected to what you are avoiding. Determine the significance and additional effects that addressing this avoidance will have on other areas of your life.

2. Once you begin to understand avoidance, the work begins. A lot of growth can happen when you address the emotional impact a situation has on you. This usually involves both internal and external work. I encourage you to start with internal first. The internal work involves the way you define and describe your experience. The event or situation itself is long over, but how you replay it furthers the experience for you. Learn to focus on what you have learned or become because of the situation. Instead of saying it was the "worst thing that could have ever happened," learn to say that because you went through it, you are stronger or you can see just how resilient you can be. External resolutions come with changing how you interact with a situation or setting. Maybe you had a bad experience at one of your favorite locations, and now, it's a constant reminder of bad, not good. An external resolution may come in focusing on ways to create new experiences in this place to help you reclaim them.

17
Sacrificing the Present for the Future

You might find yourself in a tug of war between your present and your future. In the present, decisions are made in the moment. "Do I eat this piece of cake?" "Do I go on this date?" "Do I purchase this item?" A decision that satisfies you in this moment may have a bigger impact on your life later on.

To make decisions about your future, it's important to consider how this decision will influence the future. For example, when determining whether or not to take a new job, you need to consider the work schedule, the commute, the pay, and the benefits. It's a decision you must make in the present, but its effects last longer than the moment the decision is made.

It is sometimes easy to minimize a single decision. "This purchase is a small one; it should not affect my savings" or "I'll go out on a date tonight because I just want to have a little fun." Then one date gives a false sense of connection that leads into another and eventually marriage. I may be whispering some truths that echo the decisions of your past. Know that you are not alone. The point is, now that you are aware, what happens moving forward becomes the work in progress.

Sacrificing the present for the future is about bringing the future impact into the decision-making process. If you prioritize the experience in the here and now, it leaves little room to value the bigger picture. It is about letting go of the benefits you might enjoy right now and seeing that there is greater value in what the decision supports in the future. Which means future benefits must be significant to you.

Tips

1. Establish the value of the future goal. If it has substance that lets you know that even though you would enjoy the "in the moment" decision, that benefit pales in comparison to what you would get if you delayed gratification.

2. Continuous connection with the future goal. It is easy to dismiss the future goal when it is not an immediate thought. This goal must show up regularly in your everyday life. It should be on your vision board, in a daily affirmation routine, notes to yourself all over the place. Whatever helps you know it has a place in your decision-making right now.

18
GUARDING YOUR VISION

If I were to step into in room with a crowd of people and ask if anyone ever dreamed about doing something, being something, experiencing something, I would get 100% of the room to raise their hands. But if I were to ask how many have accomplished that dream, the number of hands would not reach 100%. Is it because some people just are lucky? Is it that some people are born with more gifts and talents? Part of you wants to say yes, and another part of you knows there is more to it.

Dreams are a vision you have. Visions are inspired by many things that happen throughout your life, as well as your personal traits. Many people visualize homeownership, having certain jobs, or building a family. The value of why the vision is important is connected to the visionary.

When you envision something for yourself, an emotional connection happens. Excitement, fear, joy, doubt, hope, and worry. All are part of going after something—but you must be careful who you share things with. When you envision something, it is loaded with thoughts, such as "Am I good enough?" "Will I be able to hold on to it once it happens?" "What will people think of me?" You go from the picture that the vision gives you to worrying about the what-ifs and the how-tos. This is where things can shift from accomplishing a vision to sitting on it.

Let me share this thought with you. There may be times that you envision something that is either something you don't need to pursue or have time to pursue. But no matter what, the vision, the dreams you have, should be guarded. Even the ones you may never pursue.

Guarding your vision is not about locking it away. It is not about keeping it a secret. It is about being mindful of who has access to it. There is vulnerability and value that are connected to your vision. The people you let it in should be ones who can be objective to your needs, help support your development, and create accountability.

Tips

1. Understand the value of why it is important to guard your vision. There is danger in simplifying this step of going after your vision. Know it is about how you manage the experience you encounter around having a vision. Think about it. If someone is always pointing out the negatives and swing doubt, you are more likely to dismiss the thought of going after something. If someone always points out the limitations, you might always consider what you don't have versus what you do. Or it will take you longer to break through all their points of view to find your own. This happens whether it is a vision worth pursuing or not. The space you guard is yourself. Be sure to guard your vision.

2. Understand the type of people who should have access. Don't determine it by position alone. Your parents may not be the people who should have access. Your best friend may or may not be the person. Things you want to consider are based on personal traits (self-discipline, trustworthiness, objectivity), skill sets (as they relate to your vision), and their drive for success (motivations, passions, accomplishments).

19
Respecting the Process

Have you ever felt like things are taking too long to happen? Do you ever wish you could just skip a few steps and move on to the next right away? Are you eager to be done with something and see the finished product? Now I want you to think about some of your favorite foods. Ask yourself if the cook skipped a step, cooked them at a higher temperature, or stopped cooking earlier than the recipe called for. Would the dish taste the same? Would you want to eat it? Or how about the difference between sautéing the vegetables before adding them to the dish and just chopping them raw and adding them. If you know anything about cooking, you'll realize there is a flavor shift in just this step. The cooking process takes a little longer, but the end-product flavor is worth it.

Similar to the cooking process, there are things you go after that take time and effort to come to fruition. Rushing the process or removing steps can alter the outcome.

Let's expand on what happens during the process. The surface level represents the actual steps needed to accomplish a goal. You can't build a house without first laying the foundation. You can't become a doctor without going through the educational process. Each of these steps establishes the things needed for the goal to function as intended.

Another level of the process to consider is below the surface. This part of the process could be related to things like maturity. Someone could have the academic knowledge but not know how to implement that knowledge to lead others. They may need experience. Think about basketball. A player can be drafted to the NBA right out of college. He knows the game, but in the NBA, you are not only navigating the aspects of playing the game but also the business of the NBA—the shift in status. Now, in addition to the game, you are learning money management, communications skills, and more.

The other part of the process to give even less consideration is the external level—the things and people surrounding what you are doing. When a builder builds a house, they don't only consider the parameters of where they build; they also consider how what they are building influences the surrounding area and how the surrounding area will influence what is built. Sometimes the process includes developing those around you. You might be ready, but if others are not, the outcome is affected.

Tips

1. To respect the process, you must give space to understand the process you are in. The time delay or time needed relates to what must happen for the best outcome. The more you understand it, the better you can navigate your time, energy, and resources to take care of what is relevant instead of worrying about what isn't.

2. Be intentional to the three levels I highlighted in the process: the surface level, below the surface, and the external. Give value to each part to have the best outcome. Some things may not be changed but understanding them goes a long way in what you do in your process.

20
Addressing Vulnerability

Vulnerability is often viewed as something to avoid versus something to embrace. Vulnerability is viewed as unsafe versus empowering. Vulnerability is viewed as a weapon rather than a resource.

Vulnerability can be useful at times. It aids in creating so much in your life, but when you have not found a way to be vulnerable, then it transforms into something that can be damaging.

So how do you find ways to be vulnerable? First, it is about getting familiar with the vulnerable areas in your life as well as the vulnerable parts of who you are. These are things that have a level of sensitivity. You may become very protective when someone touches on them. You may withdraw from addressing them because of uncertainty. Without being aware of these vulnerabilities, it is hard to find ways to address them.

The next thing to consider is how to share your vulnerabilities safely. The hardest thing about being constructively vulnerable is that because it is unfamiliar to you, it can be difficult to explain to others. The more you learn to understand your vulnerabilities safely, the easier it becomes to share them with others.

Last, create filters to help understand when it is safe to be vulnerable. There are ways to go about this generically and other ways that might be unique to your personal experiences. A generic way could be talking to someone who can listen openly and hear what you are sharing, someone you can receive feedback from. Understand that a heated argument is not typically the space for being vulnerable. It may be triggered in this situation, but it does not usually produce space for mental and emotional support for vulnerability. It's important to be in a comfortable setting when you allow yourself to be vulnerable. There can be a difference when you are in a place that already feels safe rather than unfamiliar settings or a stressed-filled place.

As you become familiar with ways vulnerability can be resourceful, you will find yourself enjoying the many benefits it can bring to your life.

Tips

1. Know your motive for being vulnerable. Are you looking for someone to understand you better? Are you looking for ways to decrease your sensitivity or build your strength in an area of your life? Are you wanting to help yourself change for the better? Being vulnerable is not about manipulation. Being vulnerable has to come from a genuine place for yourself, others, and the situations you are vulnerable in.

2. There is a learning curve in being vulnerable, so enter into it with your expectations filtered by the perspective of growth, not perfection. For example, you may be talking to your partner about a situation that involves them. Know that they have their own thoughts and feelings regarding the situation but try and focus on your feelings in the moment, not what might be triggering them. This may not always be done perfectly, but remember, the goal is to do better to get helpful results.

21
WHAT DOES IT MEAN TO BE MORE INTENTIONAL?

I am sure along the way, I will have several conversations around the thought of being intentional. For this moment, the reflection has to do with the steps we take. We live in a fast-paced world that often requires us to do things quickly. To operate on a deadline mentality. To feel rushed and overwhelmed. The idea of one step at a time with no limits on how long it takes to master those steps might seem daunting. At least at first. But truth be told, when it comes to lasting changes, this is the way to go. Think about how many diets you have been on that are about you losing the most weight in the least amount of time. How many times did you gain that weight and then some back?

Think about how often you said you would do better at keeping your room clean. Think about the lasting effect over the weeks and months after making that commitment. And as you are probably doing already, there are countless other things you can think of where this pattern occurs.

This pattern of quick and fast doesn't make the success rate go up. So, you might begin to think, "What's the point?" or "Why should I even try?"

What if I told you that lasting change is possible if we first learn the smaller steps that are most effective for you as an individual and master one step before taking the next.

Take, for example, a skill I've mastered, one I practice daily. I make my bed every day, and for the most part, it is done in the morning. This behavior has only been shifted by the reality of being married to someone who wakes up later than me and a child I sometimes have to attend to before I can accomplish this task. For me, a bed made already shows a cleaner room because a bed is typically the biggest piece of furniture that draws your attention, and I've found that once I make the bed, I end up scanning the room for other things that are out of place.

My step of mastery was being accountable for making my bed, not cleaning my room. Making my bed had value beyond just making my bed. It became a part of starting my day. It became a part of the rest cycle in ending my day in a nicely made bed that invited me in. It became a part of starting the day with a successful task completed.

What does being intentional mean in this moment? It means steps and mastery. What is one step in the bigger picture you are looking to create? Master that before taking the next step. Stop trying to make everything about an overhaul change that is quick. Take time to make long-lasting changes you can maintain.

Tips

1. Consider the complete picture of what you are trying to do differently or better. Once you have the big picture, you can more clearly see how to create steps to change.
2. Give yourself grace. This means reflecting on how long you have been doing something or thinking something different over time. A long-lasting habit can require smaller steps to change and more time to master. Remember to give yourself grace in the process.
3. Create your steps. In the beginning, focus only on the first step. You won't begin the next step until you master the one you are on. Recognize that change will always begin at the first step. It will be a norm that no longer feels like you are starting over.

Journaling

TO LEARN MORE ABOUT ME AND FIND OUT ADDITIONAL ONLINE RESOURCES ....

Check Out

www.drquency.com

Made in the USA
Middletown, DE
26 August 2022